To Conquer

Or

Die Trying

By
Debra McLain

To Conquer Or Die Trying
By
Debra McLain

2nd Edition: 2019

Publisher Information
2nd Edition: Debra Kay McLain
dkmclain_poetess@yahoo.com

ISBN: 9781708719289
Imprint: Independently published

$9.99

Dedication

For my darling daughters

Sasha & Brittany

And those that guide me from above

Gary McLain, Sr.
Gary McLain, Jr.
David Turriff

Without you, I would have no words.

2nd Edition Revised to include a special dedication to my
twin flame, Allan Boettger, who left this realm on July 29,
2016, but will reside in my heart for eternity.
This book was for him.

Preface

When I was five years old, I used to dance around the house, pretending I was a ballerina. I would twirl and spin, without a care in the world. Those moments of joy rarely lasted long, as there was always a boogey man hiding under the bed. My mother taught me to respect my elders, do not talk back, and never question adults' actions.

A childhood of mental, physical, and sexual abuse caused a lot of anger and self-hatred. At fifteen years old, I became bulimic and anorexic. Any time I felt that my life was out of control, I turned to my eating disorder. It was always there, promising me that everything would be okay if I just followed the rules. The problem was that the rules kept changing and I lost all control.

After twenty-eight years of suffering from an eating disorder, I reached into the depths of my soul and pulled out the pain, one memory at a time. I began writing poetry as a way to release all of those words that I was not able to put a voice to.

Not long after I began my healing journey, my brother and father died within eighteen months of each other. Once again, writing poetry saved me from falling into the deep pits of depression. There were days when I could barely function. I lay on my bed sobbing uncontrollably, only to wave my white flag and surrender to the pain. During this time, I discovered that the McLain surname originated from Scotland. My ancestors were from the highland clans. The motto on the family crest reads 'Vincere Vel Mori', which is Latin for 'To Conquer or Die'. It is the perfect name for this book. With Gods help, I have conquered all of my mental demons, without dying. For this, I am grateful.

Table of Contents

Life and Death

Table of Contents . . . continued

Table of Contents . . . continued

Table of Contents . . . continued

Spirituality

Epilogue

To Conquer

Or

Die Trying

By
Debra McLain

Life and Death

A Daughters Goodbye

As the sun shines through the window,
I see you fading with each forced breath.
No longer do you grasp my hand,
or respond when I gaze into your eyes.

The smell is overpowering,
many medicines drip through your veins.
Each minute, new blood enters your body,
taking away a piece of your soul.

There is no more life in your eyes,
only a shell of what you once were.
I know it is time to say goodbye father,
this is a choice I need to make.

I lay my head upon your heart,
listening carefully as it beats.
As I place my hand upon your cheek,
it becomes clear, what must be done.

As they remove all life support,
you snore gently as if in peaceful slumber.
Have no fear, as you will not be alone,
just pay attention and you will see.

I lean closer and whisper in your ear...
It is time now daddy, "take a walk with my brother".

Freedom

The whirring sound of dialysis
brings hope to my saddened soul.
Time stands still
while waiting for answers.

Tiny hummingbirds
fly outside your hospital window.
Reminding me of your carefree days
filled with freedom of flight.

Word comes in steadily
throughout the day.
All hope of recovery has faded
along with my dreams.

There is a wretched ache in my heart
nothing will dull this pain.
I pray your soul is like the hummingbird
leaving its' nest, searching for higher ground.

Graveyard Friends

The little girl, with springy curls,
tiptoes around the headstones.
She whispers to the children,
not caring that they are bones.

Ring around the rosy,
all fall down with glee.
She runs and plays for hours,
ghostly children, she can see.

Her energy exhausted,
she sits upon a stone.
Takes out her little notebook,
and asks to be alone.

With her thoughts so vivid,
the stories fill her head.
She knows the children are not alive,
and imagines why they are dead.

Tiny girls and chubby boys,
who have died before their time.
Some are only babies,
now resting under lime.

The sun is quickly setting,
it is time to go inside.
Tomorrow is another day,
to play with children who have died.

I Am Alive

You came to me in dreamtime,
on three separate occasions.
"I am still alive"
lingered in my mind.
Confusion set in,
with each passing dream.
Could it be?
We never saw your body,
the decayed shell...
That once held your soul.
We could not bear to look,
it would have been forever
carved into our memory.
What do you mean
you are alive?
Years passed with this question
etched into my mind.
A memory came...
At once, I knew.
Heaven is real.
You are very much alive.
I can see you, hear you,
and embrace you,
during those times
when I quiet the mind
and just look, listen and feel.
You never left me,
dear brother.
So called 'death',

Cont....

is but the doorway
to being truly alive.
I feel your frequency
forever surrounding me.
Your love will never die.

Innocence Lost

Life was not gentle for the little girl,
surviving in a treacherous world.
Predators, pretending to be confidants,
her innocence devoured by lust.

Caresses, disguised as affection,
lurking in the shadows of her bedroom.
Calloused hands, hurried by intention,
invading her most sacred spaces.

Brave moments of honesty,
brought chastisement, and shame.
Reprimanded and labeled 'too sensitive',
self-hatred soon entrapped her soul.

Forever scarred with indifference,
self-inflicted wounds were far deeper and precise.
Starvation was her weapon of choice,
a longing for lungs made out of dust.

A twenty-eight-years-to-life sentence,
bars consisting of self-loathing and depreciation.
Temporary insanity, caused by social immorality,
inner demons controlling every thought and action.

Alive, but barely breathing,
existing on ice chips and determination.
Blue lips and fingernails... both signs,
that blood still pumped through icy cold veins.

Cont...

Warmth became something she longed for,
in the dark caverns of her double king bed.
Shivering felt like earthquakes to her weary bones,
chattering teeth, slamming against aching gums.

Life... the only barrier between Heaven and earth.
Starving for affection and a loving embrace,
her prayers for death went unanswered...
She was forced to live a life of self-destruction.

Living on Air

For half of my life,
I punished myself for being alive.
Starving for affection,
my body denied of nutrition,
I was not living, only existing.
Eating was against the rules.
I became a master at the game.
Purple lips and pale white skin,
meant I was winning,
even though I played alone.
Self-punishment... rewarded
by compliments and praise.
How could they know,
their words fed me?
Living on air...
A concentration camp victim,
of my own making.
My brain, the prison guard,
locking my spirit,
behind the bars of self-control.
Hunger filled my weary body.
Days of barely breathing.
A ghost... pretending to be alive.
Wanting to disappear,
in a world that only brought pain.
Anorexia was my best friend,
my confidant, my every thought.
Her torment was relentless,
telling me, I was worthless.

Cont....

I did not deserve to be alive.
She was a liar.
I found the strength...
Peace and love,
allowed me to see...
I am perfect,
in Gods eyes.
He held me in his embrace,
until I quit struggling.
Filling me with a passion,
I was denied for so long.
Self-love... my new best friend.

My Loving Guide

We had spent the day fishing,
lounging in lawn chairs by the river's edge.
A sunny and warm June day,
filled with laughter and 'remember me' moments.

The family gathered around the porch,
brought together by disturbing news.
The Devil came for a visit,
threatening our family with a gun.

You were so protective and brave,
with feet firmly on the ground.
He was angered by your fierceness,
you stopped a bullet with your heart.

Your Beloved was so frightened,
she came running to your side.
The Devil cared not, she was with child,
she stopped a bullet too.

God held you in His arms that night,
then He took you Home.
Your baby girl lies on your chest,
where she sleeps for Eternity.

You have never left me,
promising always to be my guide.
I call upon you daily,
you help me find my way.

Cont....

Those moments when I need you,
meditation quiets my mind.
I sit on a stone bench in Heaven,
and wait for you to appear.

My heart is free from sadness,
excitement fills my veins.
You always sit beside me,
and say, "I have been here all along".

My Inspiration

Life is so short,
yet we take it for granted.
It can end at any moment,
yet we live each day as if we have eternity.
My heart aches with sorrow.
This pain so real,
I can barely breathe.
You were in my life so briefly,
taken from me with such cruelty.
You were not done living.
I still needed you.
Eighteen months you were my father,
for eternity, you will be my inspiration.
Life has a way of changing,
day by day.
With each breath taken,
I will rejoice in the miracle of living.
I will be strong for you dad,
and try not to cry.
After all, we are McLain's...
Our motto is 'To Conquer or Die'.

Nowhere to Hide

She was barely eleven,
when her mama married an addict.
Heroin and alcohol consumed him,
a paranoid, controlling convict.

No longer was she allowed to play,
there were a new set of rules.
No going outside, no talking to boys,
always come straight home from school.

Shorts and jeans went in the trash,
he said she looked like a tease.
Mama bought her skirts to wear,
they had to go past her knees.

Her hair was cut 3 inches short,
which made her very sad.
Mama let him have control,
'cause she did not want him mad.

The little girl watched him shoot up,
he went from bad to worse.
Mama worked nights, was not around,
the little girl felt so cursed.

Doing chores for hours on end,
he leered at her from a distance.
One day she was doing dishes,
he was on her in an instant.

Cont....

His arms went around her from behind,
she could feel his hot breath on her neck.
Frozen in fear, she behaved as he asked,
she knew he would keep her in check.

He felt her up through her clothes,
which made her cry in fear.
With nowhere to go, she ran to her room,
sat huddled in a corner in tears.

He came in, stood guard by the door,
threatening for hours on end.
"Do not tell, or you will pay,
to an orphanage, I will send".

Mama came home late that night,
so there was no chance to share.
The very next day, she told her tale,
mama really did not care.

Every night for months on end,
he came into her room.
No other purpose, but to scare,
her life was filled with doom.

Children are abused every day,
they rely on parents to protect.
Some little children have no one,
they live a life of neglect.

Pretending

I close my eyes
and think of you.
A little boy,
running free.
Pretending to be happy,
with not a care.
Wanting to protect,
you wipe away my tears.
You try to be strong,
and tell me it will be all right.
Your eyes say otherwise,
as they attempt to hide the pain.
A household of contradiction...
Stepfather, preacher,
hypocrite, abuser.
Just smile big brother,
keep it all inside.
Someday, oh
someday you will be truly free.
God will welcome you,
into his embrace.
You will be Home,
never to pretend again.

Send Me a Sign

As you laid there dying,
were you scared?
Or were you ready,
with no cares, no fear?
I have to believe you were faithful,
as you used to be.
Always saying God would embrace you,
and love you eternally.
Your last few years were tormented,
the happy moments few.
If you had only reached out your hand,
I would have been here for you.
Death is so final.
There are no second chances.
Anger fades after time,
replaced with acceptance.
Guilt, however, can take longer,
for me it is true.
You were alone for 2 weeks,
I was not with you.
Your death made me weep,
as you already know.
I asked for a sign,
you sent me a rainbow.
A beautiful rainbow with two ends,
set upon a basin of rain.
There will never be another with such meaning,
one that washes away my pain.
My dear sweet brother,

Cont....

you knew I needed you near.
A rainbow was not enough,
so you sent me a song to hear.
'Have I told you lately that I love you',
on the radio so loud.
I knew it was another sign,
because of me, you were proud.
You were laid to rest today,
the sun was shining through the rain.
This is not goodbye my dear brother...
Someday... we shall meet again.

Unseen Scars

Fifteen years old, and all alone,
I answered the door to a friend.
He knew my family all my life,
there was no reason to defend.
He looked at me in anger,
pure hatred on his face.
Instantly afraid, I ran to my room,
putting a distance in our space.
Running to the window, I yelled in fear.
He smashed the door, and scared me so.
His breath reeked from beer, so did his clothes.
He was on me in a second, and would not let go.
Hands around my neck, and gasping for air,
my life flashed before my eyes.
Instinct kicked in, I kneed him hard,
it was not my day to die.
The police were called, they came quick.
They had only been down the road.
He had already stabbed another friend,
to the cops, my story was told.
He went to prison, for the rest of his life.
My family never saw him again.
The scars he left me were unseen,
they have burned always, from within.

When I Think of You

Mother, do you miss me,
or whisper words of love?
Do you hear my heart break,
when I think of you?

Mother, do you miss me,
or cry for me at night?
Do you feel my embrace,
when I think of you?

Mother, do you miss me,
or ever speak my name?
Do you see me in your mind,
when I think of you?

Mother, do you miss me,
or remember who I am?
Do you sense my tears,
when I think of you?

Open your heart dear mother.
Hear my cries, feel my touch.
See my soul, sense my pain.
Please, please, start missing me.

Love

Act of Nature

Gentle raindrops fall silently.
Their fragrance lingers in the air.
Silently cleansing.
The ground sings, refreshed.

The tornado reaches down forcefully.
It destroys everything in its path.
Leaving destruction.
The earth cries, devastated.

Love, like an act of nature.
One never knows...
Will it purify ones heart
or leave it in shambles?

Blackout

We have that earth moving
soul shaking kind of chemistry
that rattles my bones
and causes tremors from
the top of my head
to the very tip of my toes.

Your essence flows through
my veins and replaces
my blood with magical
sparks of energy
that threatens to blow
out city lights for miles.

Champagne Kisses

I smell his aftershave,
as he leans over the table.
For a moment,
I believe he is going to kiss me.

His whiskers,
gently touch my neck.
I shiver slightly,
as he inhales me.

Strawberry champagne,
never tasted so good.
A first date,
worthy of a poem.

Dark vs. Light

He claims to be that of darkness,
filled with rage, a flaming coal.
I see the light within his heart,
it is that, which enchants my soul.
His exhaustion makes him weary,
his profession leaves him seething.
I see dedication, a man so loyal,
a man whose valor is like breathing.
He says he is void of feeling,
heartless, and prone to depression.
I see a blank canvas, a slate wiped clean,
his life is poetry, an art by expression.
He sees his faults, a tortured soul,
his writes describe the pain.
I see his greatness, my man is a king...
Over my heart, he does reign.

Distant Love

Your smile is a thousand sunbeams,
shining light-rays upon my heart.
Your magnetism transcends the distance...
I can feel you, even though we are apart.

Earthquake

Separation, caused by a fault line of fear,
fractured by unspoken boundaries.

Aftershocks from the past,
induce tremors in my weary heart.
Energy and rapid movements,
kept under control, by fear of rejection.

Brief moments of calmness,
grant me hope of eternal tranquility.
Love... the force between two souls.
He takes my hand, we leap into the core.

Forbidden Love

A gentle kiss upon my lips,
awakes me from peaceful slumber.

Dreams are just the imagination,
playing tricks on my heart.

Oh, how I wish his love for me,
was stronger than his denial.

Forbidden love lingers on my skin,
reminding me of what cannot be.

A tear slips down my cheek,
as I drift back to sleep.

Forever Love

The old leather journal,
was tucked neatly
between the crisp, white linen.
Only two days had passed,
since she left this earthly plane.
He picked it up gently,
this newfound treasure.
Breathing in the scent of
rosemary and lavender.
With trembling hands,
he traced her delicate penmanship.
'Our Love is Forever',
inscribed on the cover.
Faded yellow pages,
filled with hopes, dreams, love.
He wept silently,
wanting to understand.
"Why have you left me, my darling?"
She placed her etheric hand,
upon his rugged face.
"I have not forsaken you, my love.
I am only behind the veil."
Sensing her presence,
he covered her hand with his.
There was no longer silence,
as he listened with his heart.
"We shall be together,
when your journey is through.
You will join me in Heaven,
never to be separated again".

31

Genie in a Bottle

I found a Genie in a bottle,
as I walked along the shore.
She granted me 3 wishes,
I dare not ask for more.

My first wish, without a doubt,
is everlasting love.
I want my soul mate in my life,
with blessings from above.

My second wish is obvious,
I want him by my side.
For him to bend, on one knee,
and take me as his bride.

My third wish is for family,
our children, to be friends.
Brothers and sisters for life,
a love that does not end.

I will not wish for money,
or a huge mansion by the sea.
My only wish for evermore,
is to have them here with me.

Heartscapes

Wrapped up in love,
on a chilly
winter morning.

The rising sun,
awakens my
memories.

Your essence,
still lingers
on my skin.

Where you wrote,
our forever
with your fingertips.

Hungry

Your love for me has awoken a hunger.
I was not even aware I was starving.
When I look into your eyes,
I can see into the depths of your soul.
Let me pull out all the broken bits,
and devour them with my desire.

Immortalized

I stare at his photograph,
memorizing every line and curve.
Every shadow tells a story,
exhaustion, pain, heartache.
His eyes hypnotize,
casting a spell upon my soul.
Lips so sensuous and soft,
teasing me with promises.
I run my finger along his jawline,
admiring his strength and courage.
My love grows stronger every day.
I hold his photograph... he holds my heart.

Insanity

The day stretches ahead of me,
like a long dark cavern.
I reach out my hands,
hoping to feel the edges of sanity.
My vision suddenly clears.
There is a rainbow.
Bright colors of wisdom...
A curtain of love upon my soul.

Let Love Flourish

I feel your love for me, of that, there is no doubt.
Your secrets come between us, truths only you know.
I know not your thoughts, only the parts you wish to share.
Instead of growing higher, our love simply plateaus.

If only love were enough, to fill this ache inside.
Emptiness and longing, seep out of every pore.
Your actions do not match your words,
I am a forbidden secret, how is it me, you adore?

I want to scream it on the rooftops,
for the entire world to hear.
"This man loves me, for who I am!
He trusts me with his heart, and will not disappear!"

The truth I know, does not set me free.
Yet, my heart holds dear, sweet whispers of love.
Words, written for your soul mate,
whom you have spent your life thinking of.

I had to set you free, for my own sanity.
You, loving me, is a wish that I hold true.
Although you give your love to many,
my love and devotion, belong, only to you.

I want it all, my darling, your love for me to keep.
No doubts, no hesitations, no paralyzing fears.
My wish is that you feel it, absorb it deep within.
Our love could last a lifetime, if you only let me near.

Cont....

Sending love, each and every day,
my faith in you, will never cease.
Although my heart breaks every moment,
I will continually pray for peace.

Live your life my love, experience what you must.
If you truly love me, our love, you will nourish.
No other will replace me, or reside within your heart.
Your love will be mine, then, our life will flourish.

Love

If love is as deep as the ocean,
and as wide as sea to sea,
I will pretend you are my captain,
I am your damsel, come rescue me!

If love is patient,
and comes in due time.
I will pretend you are my clock,
I am the hours, we are in chime!

If love is to the moon and back,
and into the galaxies so far,
I will pretend you are my astronaut,
I am your wingman, let's ride a star!

Love is . . .

Love is a feeling,
or a wound that can ache.
You can be it, or see it,
or feel when it breaks.
Love is confusing,
it can also be blind.
Sometimes it is lost,
if lucky, you find.
Love is a pleasure,
filled with emotion.
You can hide it or show it,
depends on devotion.
Love is a passion,
it can be all endearing.
Sometimes you will chase it,
occasionally, it is searing.
Love is for me,
I want it forever.
Although I am alone,
I still think I am clever.

Loves Debris

love
in the beginning
magical moments
pure happiness
heart palpitations
promises of forever

love
in the end
dead silence
tears
lifeless moments
wrapped up in a paper bag of despair

thrown into the street
to be run over by forgetfulness

Love Flows

The dam has burst around my heart,
pain poured out, a brand new start.
A love so strong, it cracked the wall,
I cast out doubt and gave it all.
Just when love began to grow,
a wall came up and blocked the flow.
The fear is not mine...
I still believe,
my heart is open to receive.
His barrier is strong, it will not break,
for a while, my heart ached.
I found the strength deep within,
love will find me once again.
No more dams, no more walls...
No more waiting for his calls.

My Beloved

Morning brings joy,
as memories rise gently to my awareness.
Even in sleep, I fear my imperfections.
My mind is put at ease,
as you whisper your truths.
I am perfect,
in the eyes of my beloved.

My Favorite Addiction

My pupils are dilated, my pulse is intense,
if I don't get my fix, I may lose my sense.
There is a hot-blooded male, he makes me want more,
he shivers me timbers, his good looks, I adore.
Pheromones shoot through me, when I hear his voice,
staying calm and collected, is no longer a choice.
His smile makes me rush, blood goes to my head,
if I do not get my drug, I soon may be dead.
He injects me with passion, till I am weak in the knees,
his love is my poison, give me more... please.

My Love is a Poet

His words are a lullaby,
sung to a newborn babe.
So endearing and gentle,
soothing her to sleep.

His words are full of hope,
to the woman all alone.
So safe and protective,
safeguarding her dreams.

His words are pure magic,
to everyone who reads.
Leaving sparkles and fairy dust,
upon the souls that weep.

His words are those of a poet,
who writes from his heart.
He reaches the masses,
through pen, paper, and thought.

Magic

Your soul
exhales
poetry,
filling my lungs
with words
of a love song
long forgotten.

Your essence
exudes
magic,
bringing down
the barriers
that have entrapped
my long dead heart.

Peaceful Dreams

Close your eyes my darling,
feel my caress upon your cheek.

Hear me whisper love songs,
I am the one you seek.

Breathe in my love,
like a warm and toasty fire.

You are no longer alone,
my soul is your desire.

Secret Love

My life was forever changed,
when to love I gave a chance.
Releasing all fears and doubts,
my heart was in a trance.

Dreams were created,
throughout the day and night.
Every thought, every wish,
had my shining white knight.

My hopes were dashed,
when I realized his fears.
He does not love me enough,
to expose love, it is clear.

The tears have been shed,
I slapped a patch on my heart.
This pain will fade in time,
with my beloved, I shall part.

Slaying Dragons

I have a knight in shining armor,
so handsome and brave is he.
For me, he would fight an army,
bringing them to their knees.

His eyes set my soul afire,
shooting flames out of my breast.
I dance and sing with faeries,
my love, he brings me happiness.

He promises that he loves me,
for now and evermore.
His passion is so evident,
love, seeps out of every pore.

I have never met a man so great,
a gentleman of valor.
Yet, every day,
I fret for him, what seems a hundred hours.

My brave knight goes off to battle,
with his tortured soul.
I try so hard, to ease his pain,
when off to war he goes.

My hanky is in his pocket,
a reminder to be kind.
He fights no battles on the ground,
they are battles of his mind.

Cont....

He slays so many demons,
but blood he does not shed.
His lovely soul is tormented,
by monsters in his head.

Exhaustion overcomes him,
leaving him weary and sad.
He is tired of hunting dragons,
and wants happiness, so bad.

I lay his head upon my lap,
every time, when he returns.
whispering promises of hope,
for his peace, is what I yearn.

The Five Senses of Crazy

I hate the way you make me feel,
when you intrude upon my dreams.
You took my heart and soul with you,
please, leave all my senses be.

I hate the way you look at me,
undressing me with a glance.
You know I melt under your spell,
please, wake me from my trance.

I hate the way you speak to me,
your voice, the music, to my song.
You know I will never forget,
how I laughed all night long.

I hate the way you smell me,
my scent, being the air you breathe.
You know I am the perfume,
sprayed on your handkerchief.

I hate the way you taste me,
my skin, salty from our love.
You know I am the craving,
you are always thinking of.

I hate the way you touch me,
my body, the canvas, to your brush.
You work your magic fingers,
making me quiver, and blush.

Cont....

All five senses are on strike,
no longer do I need, or want.
Stay out of my dreams, forever more,
quit being cruel, with all your taunts.

The Lantern

The wind screams,
causing my old oak tree,
to shed its tired branches,
and prepare for new life.

Rain pours down,
magical little tear drops,
escape the Heavens,
to wash away my pain.

Hot coffee is brewed,
aroma brings comfort.
Warmth slides down,
my parched and weary throat.

It is the perfect weather,
to pour my heart out in a poem.
Momentary comfort is found,
under a toasty blanket near the fire.

A brightly lit lantern,
sits in the window of my soul.
It will guide my lost love,
to find his way home.

Till Death Do Us Part

His gentle hands tuck the blanket,
around my weak and weary bones.
Placing a kiss upon my forehead,
he reminds me, I am never alone.

Sixty years ago, he made a vow,
to honor and cherish our love.
Till death do us part,
he promised God above.

The doctor gave disturbing news,
my health is declining fast.
Martin can no longer care for me,
in our home, this is my last.

Yesterday was Christmas,
we spent the day together.
Holding hands by the fireplace,
remembering promises of forever.

Martin goes and gets a gun,
and tells me to close my eyes.
I let a tear slip down my cheek,
as we both say our goodbyes.

My love for him will never cease,
I know he loves me so.
This final act was based on love,
he could not bear to let me go.

Cont....

To Conquer Or Die Trying

The bullet enters my heart,
and shatters my body, so frail.
He turns the gun upon himself,
"I'll see you love, behind the veil".

True Love is Forever

They fell in love under a sunset.
Colors lit up the sky, so bright.
Promises of forever.
Married by moonlight.

War, took him to a foreign land.
Letters, written from dark places.
Fear took over every thought.
His safety, she searched for traces.

Dreams of him, brought smiles.
For in them, she had hope.
Night time brought her comfort.
A sleeping mind let her cope.

A knock on the door,
at an unsuspected time.
The news she feared most,
his life, taken by a mine.

Her love came home,
his casket bearing a flag.
She placed a kiss on his lips,
gently clutching his tags.

They now circle her neck,
a hug from him, to keep.
The tears, they fall in torrents,
her grief, a cut so deep.

Cont....

Their love is so strong,
death will not change her 'forever'.
She holds onto memories.
For, someday, they will be together.

You Are My Everything

Every wish
    I never asked for
was granted by you.

Every moment
    I never wasted
was spent with you.

Every breath
    I never held
was shared with you.

Every memory
    I never forgot
was involving you.

Every dream
    I never tossed
was slept with you.

Every wish
Every moment
Every breath
Every memory
Every dream
was all about you.

Spirituality

Dreamtime Magic

Dreams are the place where my body finds peace,
the brain finds comfort, stress leaves with more ease.
While my conscious mind sleeps, and relaxation appears,
I see loved ones that have passed, and are no longer here.

My dad is my hero, the greatest man, I adore.
Many times, I need him, deep down to the core.
When he takes my hand, it gives me such chills,
no longer is he hurting, no more cancer or ills.

My only brother, a brat, who tormented me daily,
now visits me in dreamtime, to tell me he loves me.
When he gives me a smile, and great big bear hug,
I feel it deep within, his warmth is so snug.

My uncle, my protector, who gave up this earthly plane,
is now my main guide, who allows me free reign.
He gives me a promise, of undying love,
I am always protected, from an angel above.

My three main men, who left me too soon,
are always here for me, when I wish upon the moon.
When I say their names, before I fall asleep,
their love gives me comfort, my heart they do keep.

Dreams are the magic, where wonderful things dwell,
sit back for a moment, I will share more of my tales.
The other realm is so beautiful, a promising place,
where all my men live, in a wide-open space.

Cont....

To Conquer Or Die Trying

They reside in my dreams, as well as their land,
Heaven is a kingdom, so beautiful and grand.
I see the visions, they imprint in my head,
they love to remind me, they are not dead.

Whenever I need them, I only close my eyes,
listen to my heart, and believe it is wise.
For all that I wish, is true, as it seems,
I now go to sleep, and welcome my dreams.

Giving Grace

Baby kisses, little hugs,
roses blooming, ladybugs.
Rising suns, midnight moons,
road trips in the month of June.

Leather journals, pretty old books,
mountain air, streaming brooks.
Essential oils, foaming baths,
walks along a wintry path.

Pumpkin coffee, peppermint sticks,
lazy afternoons, romantic chick flicks.
Colorful scarves, Levi jeans,
these are a few of my favorite things.

I am grateful for all I receive,
life is wonderful, I do believe.
Love, family, health, worth more than gold,
thank you God, for letting me grow old.

I Am

I Am One with the Universe.
I see above this earthly plane.
The stars and planets align with healing grace.
I greet the Heavenly beings that embrace me with their love.

We are One.
He loves us for the light beings we are.
Our purpose is to radiate the grid with our shining center.
May our light be so bright that no negative thought or action will stand in our path.
Here, for the simple purpose of being our True Self.
Our light will change not only the world, but the Universe.

You are One with God.
Shine brightly Dear Ones.
Let love and compassion lead the way.
Be the light so that no one may see the darkness.
Go forth young beings and teach what you have learned.
You are the Now, the reason for Being.
You are Love.

I Am Love

I am in Love,
with life and everything around me.

My life is peaceful,
a calm that spreads to everyone I meet.

I am filled with laughter,
a joy that radiates from my soul.

My life is in harmony,
a melody is found in every situation.

I release all illusions of anger,
misunderstandings, sadness, and discord.

I am Love.
You are too.
Breathe it in.

Meditation

A long day lies behind me.
My spirit holds onto hope,
grasping for a life raft
in an ocean of chaos.

My soul yearns for serenity.
Knowing there is peace,
hiding in the valleys
of my mind.

The angels surround me.
Enveloping me in wings,
protecting me
from forces unseen.

Breathing in deeply,
my lungs inhale
wildflowers
on a warm summer day.

A waterfall flows beside me,
washing away
the dirty soil
of an overused mind.

Sunlight shines brightly,
creating a spark
of energy
reigniting the flames of hope.

Cont....

Love enters my body.
Pink rays dancing
and swaying to music
only I can hear.
My soul is set free.
Life is but a canvas,
the paintbrush
is in my mind.

Meet Me in the Meadow

I relax my mind and meditate,
every night before I sleep.
He meets me in the meadow,
in flowers, two feet deep.

I ask him to be honest,
to his own self be true.
He admits his love for me,
his earthly body too.

He tells me that he is frightened,
to give his love away.
In the past, he has been rejected,
fear keeps his love at bay.

I touch his face, so he can feel,
the electricity as we merge.
It travels from my soul to his,
and gives us both a surge.

He puts my hands upon his heart,
tells me he will be true.
I thank him for the love he gives,
smiling, because he loves me too!

It is time to leave this space,
and return to the other plane.
I know that he is always here,
when to sleep I put my brain.

Soul Speak

You write me love songs,
disguised as poetry.
Each verse is a promise,
only I can sing.

You whisper, "I love you",
without saying a word.
Every breath is a message,
only I can inhale.

You send me the world,
in each little thought.
Every smile is a rainbow,
only I can wear.

Thank you my love,
for sharing your soul.
Every minute is a painting,
only we can create.

Epilogue

Debra McLain

About the Author

Debra McLain resides in California. She is mother to two daughters and three granddaughters. She works in agriculture, although her passion is in writing. Her dream is to publish a best seller regarding her twenty-eight year battle with an eating disorder and the spiritual awakening that followed.

Printed in Great Britain
by Amazon